BLOOD, SWEAT & BEARS

Text copyright© 1976 Stanley Burke
Drawings copyright© 1976 by Roy Peterson

Canadian Cataloguing in Publication Data

Burke, Stanley, 1923—
    Blood, sweat and bears

ISBN 0-88894-117-X

1. Hockey—Canada—Anecdotes, facetiae,
      satire, etc.
2. Canadian wit and humor.   I. Peterson, Roy.
II. Title.
GV847.2.B87   796.9'62'0971   C76-016062-7

Cover design by Roy Peterson
Design and production co-ordination by
Mike Yazzolino

J.J. Douglas Ltd.
1875 Welch Street, North Vancouver
Canada V7P 1B7

Printed and bound in Canada

BLOOD, SWEAT & BEARS

STANLEY BURKE
ROY PETERSON

J.J. Douglas Ltd.
Vancouver

The only thing that really mattered in the Swamp was Hockey.

This was the marvellous game which the animals played on the ice and this was the reason, they were sure, that God had created the long Swampian winter. And the reason He gave the Swamp Creatures those unique qualities of mind, muscle, and spirit which led them to create the game in the first place and then to be the best in all the world at playing it.

It was the Swamp's contribution to civilization.

The Creatures also invented a wonderful game called Football, with its Great Green Cup, which did so much to unite the Swamp. This was a game played on the grass in the meadow, where the animals lined up and charged one another, very much like politicians. It was a fine game but, although it started in the Swamp, it had been more or less taken over by the Eagles and was not nearly as important as Hockey.

Then there was Hoop-Ball, which the Swamp Creatures also invented, and another really smashing game called The Cross—because of the way the players crucified one another.

Of all these games which the Swamp Creatures created, Hockey and The Cross were the ones which best expressed their personality, and they were proud that these were the only games in all the world in which violence was not just condoned but actively encouraged.

They felt that this was sure proof of their virility and animalness.

And there were other nice things in the Swamp, too. There was a game called Socker, and there was swimming, and in the summer they had races in the meadow.

And once they had the Great Global Games in Mont Trial. These games were supposed to reflect the highest aspirations of the animal spirit, and the Swamp Creatures looked forward to them very much. In the end, though, they were a little disappointed, mostly because there seemed to be as many Politicians playing as Athletes, and all the Politicians were mad at each other.

The Cheetahs were mad at the Kiwis, so all the Cheetahs left.

The Camels were mad at their cousins, the Dromedaries, and there were fears that they might start fighting again. So there were guard animals everywhere.

Everybody was mad at the Ostriches, who lived to the south of the Cheetahs, and they weren't allowed to come.

And no one knew who should represent the Pekineses, the most numerous of all the animals, so they weren't there either.

But, in spite of all that, there were some exciting performances.

Mayor Jean Zappo of Mont Trial, one of the world masters at hop-jump-and-skip, put on an unbelievable display; but even he was not quite at the top of his form, as he had become slightly pregnant.

In the Political Games, the team from Nottalot, the capital of the Swamp, showed footwork which astounded the world. Putting a foot in here, a foot in there—sometimes both feet at once—Team Nottalot showed a fast-changing style of play which had the crowd on its feet, roaring.

Even the great *New Yak Times* commented editorially on Team Nottalot's brilliant double-cross play, and said that "The games may never be the same again."

High praise indeed!

And, of course, the Ordinary Animals were not forgotten, and a great lottery was arranged so they could have the fun of paying for it all.

It was exciting—all those muscly young animals running, and jumping, and throwing things—but, when it was over, many felt that there were other things they would rather have spent a billion clams on.

Hockey, for example.

After all, Hockey was what the Swamp had been about ever since that glorious day when the game had been invented by Fossil Spewitt.

As you remember, children, Fossil Spewitt was walking along the St. Florence river that wonderful winter's day long, long ago, when he saw a bunch of Beavers and Frogs out on the ice hitting each other over the head with sticks. In a flash of genius, he saw that this poetry in motion captured the essential spirit of the Swamp.

And he saw that money could be made out of it.

"This can be the binding force to build a mighty Swamp," he cried, speaking even more rapidly than usual.

But he realized that the game must first be tidied up, so he invented the puck, which helped the players to know who to hit and helped the spectators to follow the violence.

Then he invented skates, which increased the speed of the violence beyond that of any other sport.

The essential game had been born...

Fossil Spewitt had found his destiny...

And so had the Swamp.

All that remained was to add money, so Fossil Spewitt set forth to find entrepreneurs.*

He went into the wide world with his wonderful idea and soon he came upon an intelligent young Beaver called Clarence Cowbell.

*Entrepreneur is a Frog word meaning "Between takers," because an entrepreneur can stand in the middle and take from both sides and get richer than anybody.

"Clarence Cowbell," he said, "I have invented a wonderful game called Hockey which can be the binding force to build a mighty Swamp. Now I need an organizer to organize some entrepreneurs."

"Capital! Capital!" said Clarence Cowbell. "I know just the right people!"

So he took Fossil to meet two ambitious young animals named Harold Ballast and Con Smite who immediately agreed to build a Hockey Shrine called Maple Tree Gardens, so-named because it would rise up as a symbol for all the Swamp, and because of all the green stuff which would grow there.

Then Clarence Cowbell took him to meet young John Bassethound, who was at that time merely the editor of the Mont Trial *Gazette*.

"When I am grown up," said John Bassethound, "I will move to Beaverville and convince the Eatins to join me in great enterprises. And some day I shall own the Maple Tree hockey team."

And sure enough, as soon as John Bassethound had grown up, he went to Beaverville and made friends with the Eatins, and soon he owned a newspaper. Then he created a lot of wonderful magic lanterns which he placed all over the Swamp and called CTV, standing for Clam Television.

And finally, true to his promise of long ago, he acquired the Maple Trees.

...and the Preservative Party.

John Bassethound, the poor but honest young animal from West Mound, had arrived at the Summit of the Swamp. Truly a success story like something out of *Horatio Algae*.

Meanwhile Fossil Spewitt and Clarence Cowbell and Harold Ballast and Con Smite had arrived too...

And so had the Swamp.

The Swamp created Hockey. And Hockey created the Swamp.

But, in so doing, Hockey laid heavy responsibilities on every parent, every teacher; indeed, on every loyal Swampian: a duty which they gladly accepted.

"Eat up your poplar bark, Tusker, or you won't grow up to have a slap shot like Bobby Ore," a Swamp Mother would say, hoping, like all mothers, that her little animal would grow up to be like the Great Goldmine on Skates.

No effort was too great for the Swamp parents. In the middle of the night, at 50 below zero (3⅞ degrees on the new Confusius Scale) they would take their young to the Hockey ponds. The most dedicated of all these were the Jockstrap Mothers, whose voices could be heard shrilling through the pre-dawn darkness encouraging their sweet children.

"Hit him again, Butcher!" they would shout. "Hit him quick before he gets up!"

It was enough to bring tears to the eyes of every true Swampian, and to the eyes of many young players.

It was noble and, as Fossil Spewitt had foreseen long ago, it was the essence of Swampness.

Touching scenes like this were repeated thousands of times across the Swamp as an entire race of animals grew up in the heroic tradition of Hockey.

And all this was thanks to the All-Swamp Hockey League which Clarence Cowbell created as a great patriotic enterprise. You see, children, every player in the Swamp, no matter how young, no matter how obscure, was enrolled in this great democratic institution whose sole purpose was to produce future champions. Every young Swampian could thus dream that some day he might be that ultimate creature, a hockey star—unlike young Eagles, for example, who could hope for nothing better than to be a Chief Eagle like Gerald Thud.

The AHL was joined in this great work by local business animals who put the names of their companies on the players' sweaters: Joe's Poplarburgers; Swamp Shops; Devva Station Logging Company; Kickbacque Dredging Company. This helped the players, at a tender age, to realize that the purpose of Hockey, like the purpose of the Swamp, was to make money.

"A fast puck makes a fast buck," the young animals were told on one memorable occasion by the great Gordie Howl himself.

Little Basher Beaver was one of thousands of young animals growing up in this great tradition.

He remembered so well the wonderful day when, as a beginner in the Wobbler Division, with Kickbacque proudly emblazoned on his sweater, he was pushed on to the ice with his father's words ringing in his ears:

"Now get out there and *hit* somebody!"

To maintain such traditions, the All-Swamp Hockey League organized schools which helped young players like Basher to develop into proud defenders of the Swampian Way of Life.

But they were warned that there were Do-Gooders and other weaklings who undermined the highest things that the Swamp stood for: building dams, cutting down trees, making clams and, above all, playing Hockey in the great animal-like tradition of the AHL.

These traitors lost no opportunity to embarrass the government and to shake the confidence of the Ordinary Animals in their leaders. The least little thing was blown up out of all proportion—the discussions over the use of the Frog language by the canal controllers; the dredging fuss when it was claimed that some animals cleaning up in the canals were taking out a bit more than anyone had realized.

Or all that nonsense just because the players went into the stands to kick things around with the fans.

Or the charges against Dan Baloney simply because he battered somebody's head against the ice.

Then there was that time Marc Tar-Baby got hit from behind and suffered a little skull damage.

Hockey players *like* that sort of thing.

The fans like it.

And it helped to develop the basic animal instincts of the Swamp.

"Hockey is violence!" thundered Clarence Cowbell. "The Swamp is violence!"

Then, with a chuckle, he would add, "And anyway, Animals will be Animals!"

In the Hockey school, Basher and his friends were given many inspirational addresses and useful courses to help them to grow up in this true Swampian Way. There was advanced mathematics, including six-digit contractual equations used to calculate Hockey salaries. And sometimes, just for fun, they would pretend to be some great star like Gordie Howl and use a *seven*-digit equation to work out a *million-clam* contract.

UP THE CREEK
KEN DAMSEA

Basher also learned famous formulae such as Pie R², which was used to calculate the take from each game. In this formula, Pie represented the Gate and R the Rakeoff from advertising.

Then there was the Pie-Stagger-Us theorem used to calculate the total season's cut for each team—sums so great that Basher and his little friends could hardly imagine them; sums going to build a greater future.

Basher loved it all—every hour of every day. In particular he liked the evenings around the campfire when they sang such wonderful songs as the anthem of Swampian Hockey, "Gory, Gory Hallelujah."

But most of all he loved the sessions on tactics.

How to Cut Down the Odds—the odd enemy player.

Penalty Killing: how to kill an opponent without getting a penalty.

Two On One and the Fast Break: Here they learned how two attackers could hit one defender and, in the twinkling of a hip and a shoulder, put him out for the season. Executed with speed and precision, and screened from the referee, this was one of the most satisfying manoeuvres in Hockey.

And finally there were the happy hours when veterans gave the youngsters the benefit of their years of campaigning.

"The goalie wears 35 pounds of equipment," the forceful Eddie Shock told them once. "Every inch of his body is protected except his Adam's apple. Now what do you shoot for?"

"His Adam's apple!" the little voices shrilled.

Oh happy days! Happy days!

Youth, comradeship, and aggression blended in the Great Swampian Way.

The True Swamp Strong and Free.

Of course, like all good things, it had to end and, after the final year, the successful students received their coveted diplomas.

But, for the favoured few, there would be an even greater honour.

A letter.

And Basher received such a letter. On the envelope it said, "Beaverville Snarlboroughs."

Was it possible?

His paws trembled as he opened it...

and there were the magic words:

"You have been scouted by the Snarlies and in our opinion have the capability of playing for our organization.

"Our training camp is snuggled in the hills north of Beaverville," the letter continued, "only five minutes from the nearest hospital. We have planned a bang-up program and we hope you will be there."

Oh joy! Oh joy!

Scouted by the Snarlies, the greatest team in the Junior Swampian League.

And the Snarlies accepted him. He was IN.

This was it...the beginning of the Big Time.

And sure enough, his dream began to unfold just as he had imagined long ago.

He became a sensation.

Sports writers began to take an interest in him.

One wrote an article calling him "Bash the Flash, the Rookie Wonder."

Dick Bedpan of the *Goad & Flail* nicknamed him "Slash-Bash."

All his life Basher had looked on sports writers and commentators as gods. Now, here they were, writing about *him*, and he was sitting in bars with them and they called him by name, and he could buy them as many rounds of Bullrush Juice as they wanted.

"Why, they're just like ordinary animals," he said to himself.

Indeed, some were extraordinarily ordinary.

As he got to know them better, he began to realize their importance to the Swamp, and to appreciate their tireless dedication. Ordinary news-animals were always carping and criticizing, but the sports-animals were positive thinkers whose motto was "Boost, don't knock." He saw that the sports industry and, indeed, the Swamp itself, could not exist without them.

In particular, he was inspired by the enthusiasm and freshness of their language. Some of the old-timers could describe an entire game without once using ordinary words like goal, puck, or period.

"At 3:01 of the first stanza, the Big Itch bulged the hemp for his first tally," one of the Masters would write. "He bent the twine...drilled the disc...he hammered...he registered."

Never did he simply shoot or check or score.

But the really big thrill was meeting animals like Fossil Spewitt, Junior, from the All-Swamp Broadcasting Corporation, because they were the ones, of course, through their famous Hockey Night in the Swamp broadcasts, who made it all possible.

And they were the ones whose years of experience gave the fans* insights into the game which they could gain in no other way.

"The reason the Swampiens are winning," Fossil Spewitt, Junior, might observe, "is because they are shooting the puck more often and this increases their odds on scoring."

And, not to be outdone, the other commentator would reply:

"Right, Fossil. And Kenny Dry-Den is stopping the puck more often than the other goalie."

---

*Fans—from the Frog, *fanatique,* meaning "an enthusiast."

It was in these Hockey broadcasts, paid for as a patriotic service by companies such as Imperious Oil and Moleson's Bullrush Juice, that the All-Swamp Broadcasting Corporation rose to its full stature as the great uniting force of the Swamp.

Hockey and the ABC, working as a team to build a better Swamp.

And Basher knew that he was part of it.

Visitors, though, sometimes had difficulty understanding it all. They were surprised, for example, when the Creatures played their national anthem— "O Swamp"—at Hockey games. Where the visitors came from, you see, national anthems were reserved for special occasions like wars. Which just showed how little they understood Hockey.

Basher remembered one time when a distinguished visitor was watching the Snarlies obliterate some unfortunate opponents.

"Why is it," he asked, "that the Swamp Creatures try to be peacekeepers to the world while they make war at home?"

His host, who was a professor or something and understood these things, replied:

"We fight so much on the ice that we have no hatred left for anyone else. It makes us ideal peacekeepers."

Basher thought that was very interesting. Not only was Hockey helping the Swamp, it was building a better world.

This made him prouder than ever.

Life was good.

He was scoring goals...sports animals were writing about him... and girl Beavers with increasing frequency were calling to suggest that he drop around for a bit of overtime.

But then it happened...

He was HIGHJACKED.

By the Eagles.

The Eagles, you see, had acquired a taste for Hockey, and now Eagle scouts were everywhere.

In the skies.

In the trees.

In the bushes.

Just waiting for young players like "Slash-Bash." A hat trick or two, a few shoutouts, battering a few opponents through the boards—and down would swoop the scouts.

And off would go the hapless player away to the south to the Land of the Eagles.

Now it was happening to Basher.

He was carried off to play for a team called the Boll Weevils in a place which he had never heard of.

Here everything was different, and Basher was very homesick.

The animals talked in a different way.

"Yall sho got a funny-lookin woke-in stick theah."

What did it mean?

And the animals behaved in a different way.

For example, there were police Eagles everywhere...and they all carried big sticks and they swaggered.

And everywhere there were Soldier Eagles and Sailor Eagles.

But apparently there weren't enough of them, because there were billboards everywhere urging still more young Eagles to become soldiers and sailors.

"Go to distant lands," the advertisements said. "Meet fascinating people. And eliminate them."

However, these fighting animals were all peaceloving, the Eagles said.

And, to prove it, their foreign minister, Henry Kiss'n-Grr, would have them fly over from time to time and declare peace on someone.

This made the Eagles feel better. And probably explained why they liked Hockey so much even if they didn't understand it.

But Basher wasn't too sure about the Eagles' peacekeeping. They seemed to overdo it a bit, and someone was bound to get hurt.

And there were other things he didn't like.

He didn't like it, for example, when two teams of Swampians had to line up before the playoffs for the Alswamp Cup—named for Lord Alswamp—and listen to Kate Sniff belt out "God Bless Our Eagle Land."

But, on the other hand, it meant that young players like himself could break into the Big Time and earn unbelievable amounts of money.

Back home with the Snarlies, he got only 60 clams a month. Now suddenly he was making *6,000* a month!

Of course, although he was playing for an Eagle team, the Civil Serpents in Nottalot had ways of wrapping themselves around a lot of his hard fought-for money.

But Basher knew how desperately the Swamp needed those clams. You see, when he was playing for the Snarlies, a teacher sometimes gave them classes—the Snarlies were "Big on Education"—and they used to read *Mapleleaf* magazine and *Readers Digress* and *Slime* too, until it disappeared. In the classes they learned that only Hockey could provide the clams that the Swamp needed to survive.

Clams to meet the just demands of strikers.

Clams to pay the Civil Serpents to learn the Frog language.

Clams to pay Bureaucrabs* to administer the All-Swamp Broadcasting Corporation.

Clams to pay someone like Berry Plumtree, who had worked so hard to get food prices down. And to pay Eugene Flailem to make sure they stayed up.

---

*Named because of their ability to make progress while going sideways.

Basher was proud of the way the Hockey industry responded to this crisis, working harder than ever to maximize profits and save the Swampian Way of Life.

No franchise was left unturned.

No licence unlicenced.

No market unmarked.

Ten thousand products were authorized to carry the insignia of the All-Swamp Hockey League, a statesmanlike move which brought revenue to the league and made the public aware of the vital role of Hockey. There were fur cream ads—"For the wet look, use Beaver Oil;" or "Don't look like a drip. Swamp Creme." There were clever ads for AHL toupees starring Bobby Bull—"No-scratch, perfect-match new thatch for your bald patch!"

The Swamp Oil companies joined the campaign and ran important announcements during the Hockey broadcasts telling the animals not to worry about running out of oil.

"As fast as you can use it up, Imperious will find more," the announcer would say in an important voice. Then, stirring music would play and the announcer would point out how patriotic it was to make big profits.

It made Basher proud to be part of all this.

But most of all, he was proud of the way his fellow players rose to the challenge by pushing their earnings to new levels of idealism.

Bobby Ore, in spite of failing knees, was prepared to sacrifice himself playing for the Blackbirds to bring in five million clams.

Gordie Howl and his legendary sons continued to make history with their own million-clam goldmine in the desert.

Bobby Bull made a million playing for the Win-a-Pack Jabs.

Phil Expose-His-Toe went over 500,000 playing for the Bust 'Em Bruise'Ems before going to the New Yak Dangers.

And then there was Ken Dry-Den, with the Swampiens, who received his name when he finally got a raise to 250,000 and was able to afford a new house.

So, from all these patriotic sources, the clams rolled in, the Swamp seemed once again secure, and Peter Waterhole, the Chief Minister, thought he might go out to the west and have fun on the Otter Slides. He was quite good at this.

But then a new and more frightening danger arose, a challenge to the Honour of the Swamp itself. You see, for some years the Swampians had been teaching the other animals to play Hockey.

It was the Swamp's civilizing mission to the world. And eventually, some of them became quite good, especially the Bears.

Then one day a message arrived from the Bears. Would Team Swamp accept a challenge? The Swamp Creatures were amused at the Bears' presumption and gladly accepted. This was something new, and there was intense curiosity as a supremely confident Team Swamp took to the ice. Would the Swamp win *all* the games, or just most of them?

"Bears can't hit," said Fossil Spewitt, Junior. "Right, Fossil," said the other commentator, "and they don't like to get hit themselves."

But, in the end, it was the Swamp that was hit. Right in its pride.

Because the series turned out to be almost a disaster, with Team Swamp's winning goal coming only in the last 30 seconds.

It was a close thing, but the Swampians explained it by reminding everyone that they did not have all their best players. And by admitting that they had been overconfident. But anyway, it was a victory. With moments of high drama.

Who could forget the time when Allan Eagleclaw, overcome with emotion, rushed on to the ice to wave fraternal greetings to the Bear fans?

The Bears, touched by his typically Swampian gesture, roared back.

Then the Swampians gave a unique response which would make them ever-remembered in the annals of Bearish sport. Having no flowers to throw, the quick-witted Swampians threw the seats instead.

The Bears were deeply moved and observed that, in their long history, nothing like it had ever been seen before. The Bear press referred to the Swampians as *hooligani*, an expression of endearment meaning high-spirited and full of life.

And so the Swamp Creatures went home content with their victory and in the realization that their sport, and their sportsmanship, had helped to build bridges of understanding with the Bears.

But they resolved to be more careful next time.

There was no doubt about it. Bears could play Hockey.

The two series which followed, however, proved more disquieting than the first and the Swamp Creatures began to doubt their virility and their very animalness itself.

Their purpose in life seemed to be slipping away.

Only one thing could restore their confidence and their honour. An impeccable victory over the best teams in the world: the Bears, the Yerpians—so called because they came from Yerp, and the Eagles.

NOT A GAME MUST BE LOST.

A flawless team. A flawless dream.

And so, two years were spent in preparation.

A secret training camp was built far from the eyes of foreign spies.

New assault tactics were worked out with the assistance of the Swampian Army.

Most important of all, all the Swamp's best players came back from the land of the Eagles especially for the challenge.

Thanks to the genius of the Swampian Research Council and the advertising agencies, they were able to alter the minds of players to create a new bio-dynamic breed of animals who thought of only one thing—*victory*.

And money.

These were the animals who made up the Ultimate Team Swamp—and Basher was one of its stars.

So the Moment of Truth arrived—the series for the new Swamp Cup, emblematic of global supremacy; the Swamp Cup which would prove who were the better animals, which was the superior Way of Life.

Anxious eyes were glued to the magic lanterns as the series opened with the playing of "O Swamp" and with Peter Waterhole's ringing declaration "We Shall Overcome!"

And, in the end, they were relieved and delighted when Team Swamp won over the Bears,
   the Eagles,
      the Speeds,
         the Spins,
            and the Checks.

It was good, but once they were beaten—by the Checks. And, even more serious, they didn't have a chance to prove themselves against the best of the Bears. The Bears arrived, in fact, with a team of untried cubs who didn't do well at all and their grouchy coach explained that they were training for the real championships later in Yerp.

But the series as a whole was exciting. Especiallly the last game when the tie-ing goal was scored by Bill Barbarous and then, in overtime, the winner was fired by Darrell Sizzler past the sensational Check goalie whose name was Gorilla—because he filled the goal and his huge arms reached out and stopped everything.

But the Swamp's goalie, Rogue-y Bash-On, was equally good and was rewarded with a little cart in which he could ride around the Swamp.

And Bobby Ore was a hero and everybody loved that.

And the Creatures loved their new friends, the Checks, and gave them a great cheer.

Earlier, you see, they had rather overlooked the Checks and about all they knew was that they lived at the edge of some mountains called the Yalps where they sang and danced and played hockey.

It seems that the Bears, too, were fond of these Little Brothers and from time to time would come over the mountains to visit.

This excited the Checks very much and they would throw flowers and things at the visitors.

And they would play hockey with them as a way of showing their appreciation.

So everyone was pleased when the Checks played well in the Swamp Tournament and all the Creatures went home reasonably content.

Except Allan Eagleclaw.
"We haven't won," he said. "We haven't won until we beat the Bears."

"The *real* Bears."

"Why did they leave their stars at home?"

Then it hit him. Like Bobby Bull's slapshot.

The Bear stars were ready to jump!

He could buy them!

Suddenly he saw it all—clear and shimmering like the ice on Lake Inferior.

The Eagleclaw Plan for Total Domination Forever!

Eyes glittering wildly, he rushed to Nottalot for an emergency meeting with the cabinet.

The Ministers were delighted to see someone with an idea—any idea.

"Eagleclaw. Eagleclaw. What shall we do?" they cried.

"First we buy back Team Swamp from the Eagles, "he began, one paw thrust Napoleonically into his jacket.

At the other end of the table, he could see Peter Waterhole's eyes beginning to glitter in response.

"But how would we pay for them?" said Marc La Ponde, who was supposed to know something about sport. "We'd have Bobby Ore playing for someone like the Flim Flam Flyers."

"Give him Flim Flam," cried Allan Eagleclaw.

The ministers were thunderstruck.

What audacity! What genius!

Next, Eagleclaw organized a great rally in Maple Tree Gardens which was carried live by the All-Swamp Broadcasting Corporation and by Clam Television. He introduced the Chief Minister after carefully briefing him on what to say.

"We shall fight them on the beaches, on the mud flats, in the bullrushes," cried Allan Eagleclaw.

"If the Swamp shall last for a thousand years, let them say this was their finest hour!" cried Peter Waterhole.

The animals sprang cheering to their feet.

And, across the Swamp, a new wave of hope and pride swelled in every animal.

The Swamp Creatures rallied as never before. Here was something that really mattered!

Beavers and Frogs forgot their differences. Even René Terrifique, the radical Frog leader, went to Nottalot to help Peter Waterhole in this, his finest hour.

And John Turnover came back to take up the financial reins of the Swamp.

From the western meadow, Peter Lowspeed announced that the Gophers would send unlimited amounts of Swamp Oil—at the old price.

And Bill Bendit, the Otter leader, sent word across the Great Hills that he was sending huge quantities of fish and advice.

From one end of the Swamp to the other, the Ordinary Animals responded with almost frenzied enthusiasm, often donating their most precious possessions: wedding rings; curling trophies. One or two hockey players even donated their royalties.

Clams piled up, and soon Peter Waterhole was able to announce that Team Swamp was COMING HOME.

Not just for a single series, but for good. Forever.

There was music. Dancing in the meadow.

Charles Grynch, the old war correspondent, wrote that even at the end of the Great Animal War, there were no scenes of equal joy.

But this was only part of the story.

Even as the Swamp celebrated, the candles were burning in the East Lodge as Allan Eagleclaw masterminded the ultimate coup...

...the most daring undercover operation in the history of the world: Operation Bearbait—to arrange *the defection of the entire Bear Team!*

It was organized in highest secrecy by Allan Eagleclaw, Peter Waterhole and Commissioner Truncheon of the Royal Swampian Mounted Police.

It would cost a lot of clams, but anything was justified to save the Swamp.

Allan Eagleclaw himself would be the secret agent to arrange the Great Defection, with authority from John Turnover to offer contracts up to one hundred thousand clams to dazzle the Bear players.

He first approached Valeriy Kall-Em-Off, the greatest of the Bear stars.

"A hundred thousand clams!" said Eagleclaw, his eyes sparkling.

"You got to be kiddink," said Kall-Em-Off.

Eagleclaw was uncertain. Had he offered too much? Had he offended the Bear's ideals of animal equality?

He quickly got the answer as Kall-Em-Off muttered something about "not enough to pay taxes even," and started to amble away.

"Two hundred thousand," shouted Eagleclaw.

Kall-Em-Off kept ambling.

"Five hundred thousand," shouted Eagleclaw wildly.

Kall-Em-Off paused and turned. "Ven Sanderblast gets a million for nuddink?"

Finally, Kall-Em-Off sat down, tossed back two more shots of Bear-juice, and signed for ten million plus the town of Callgirlie.

But now Eagleclaw was out of clams. One player signed up and he was broke.

A courier was dispatched to Nottalot, where John Turnover rushed out and floated a new bond issue which put the Swamp back in the game.

With renewed energy, Eagleclaw returned to the attack and soon lined up Alexsandr Yak-You-Shove, the Bears' top scorer, for five million plus Churchmouse Falls, half of Nottalot, and a lifetime supply of Bear-juice.

Vladislav Trek-Yak, the miraculous Goalie, went for four million plus ten thousand acres of tundra and the town of VanSnoozer—the Otters would understand. After all, they were beginning to play surprisingly good Hockey.

So finally, it was done.

He had given away the Swamp, but the entire Bear team had been signed up and smuggled out disguised as a You-Cranium dance troupe.

The Swamp Creatures went mad.

A huge crowd gathered to greet the Bears with booze and bearhugs. Girl animals bombarded them with flowers, kisses, themselves.

Then Peter Waterhole embraced Allan Eagleclaw, tears streaming down his cheeks.

"You have done what no other animal could do," he cried. "I ask you, Allan Eagleclaw, to become the new Chief Minister of the Swamp!"

The crowd gasped. . .then roared its approval.

"And you, Peter Waterhole, must be our Governor General!" cried Eagleclaw.

The crowd went wild and surged forward to carry the two animals in triumph into the blazing night; a night of wild jubilation, bonfires, magnificent madness.

But when euphoria was at its height, it happened.

Across the network of the All-Swamp Broadcasting Corporation, an unknown face* told the Swamp:

"BOTH TEAMS HAVE BEEN BOUGHT BY THE CAMELS!"

*It would have been Lloyd Blanderson but he, too, had been bought.